IF YOU FAIL TO PLAN,
YOU ARE PLANNING TO FAIL.
- BENJAMIN FRANKLIN

IF LOST PLEASE CONTACT:

_____

_____

RECEIVE A FREE GIFT
WHEN YOU SUBSCRIBE TO OUR
MAILING LIST AT

WWW.ELLEJOY.NET

2022

JANUARY 2022

S	M	T	W	T	F	S
26	27	28	29	30	31	1
2	3	4	5	6	7	8
9	10	11	12	13	14	15
16	17	18	19	20	21	22
23	24	25	26	27	28	29
30	31					

FEBRUARY 2022

S	M	T	W	T	F	S
30	31	1	2	3	4	5
6	7	8	9	10	11	12
13	14	15	16	17	18	19
20	21	22	23	24	25	26
27	28	1	2	3	4	5

MARCH 2022

S	M	T	W	T	F	S
27	28	1	2	3	4	5
6	7	8	9	10	11	12
13	14	15	16	17	18	19
20	21	22	23	24	25	26
27	28	29	30	31	1	2

APRIL 2022

S	M	T	W	T	F	S
27	28	29	30	31	1	2
3	4	5	6	7	8	9
10	11	12	13	14	15	16
17	18	19	20	21	22	23
24	25	26	27	28	29	30

MAY 2022

S	M	T	W	T	F	S
1	2	3	4	5	6	7
8	9	10	11	12	13	14
15	16	17	18	19	20	21
22	23	24	25	26	27	28
29	30	31	1	2	3	4

JUNE 2022

S	M	T	W	T	F	S
29	30	31	1	2	3	4
5	6	7	8	9	10	11
12	13	14	15	16	17	18
19	20	21	22	23	24	25
26	27	28	29	30	1	2

JULY 2022

S	M	T	W	T	F	S
26	27	28	29	30	1	2
3	4	5	6	7	8	9
10	11	12	13	14	15	16
17	18	19	20	21	22	23
24	25	26	27	28	29	30
31						

AUGUST 2022

S	M	T	W	T	F	S
31	1	2	3	4	5	6
7	8	9	10	11	12	13
14	15	16	17	18	19	20
21	22	23	24	25	26	27
28	29	30	31	1	2	3

SEPTEMBER 2022

S	M	T	W	T	F	S
28	29	30	31	1	2	3
4	5	6	7	8	9	10
11	12	13	14	15	16	17
18	19	20	21	22	23	24
25	26	27	28	29	30	1

OCTOBER 2022

S	M	T	W	T	F	S
25	26	27	28	29	30	1
2	3	4	5	6	7	8
9	10	11	12	13	14	15
16	17	18	19	20	21	22
23	24	25	26	27	28	29
30	31					

NOVEMBER 2022

S	M	T	W	T	F	S
30	31	1	2	3	4	5
6	7	8	9	10	11	12
13	14	15	16	17	18	19
20	21	22	23	24	25	26
27	28	29	30	1	2	3

DECEMBER 2022

S	M	T	W	T	F	S
27	28	29	30	1	2	3
4	5	6	7	8	9	10
11	12	13	14	15	16	17
18	19	20	21	22	23	24
25	26	27	28	29	30	31

JANUARY 2022

Sunday	Monday	Tuesday	Wednesday
26	27	28	29
2	3	4	5
9	10	11	12
16	17 Martin Luther King Day	18	19
23	24	25	26
30	31		

JANUARY 2022

Thursday	Friday	Saturday	Notes
30	31	1 New Year's Day	
6	7	8	
13	14	15	
20	21	22	
27	28	29	

FEBRUARY 2022

S	M	T	W	T	F	S
30	31	1	2	3	4	5
6	7	8	9	10	11	12
13	14	15	16	17	18	19
20	21	22	23	24	25	26
27	28	1	2	3	4	5

Notes

Goals & Priorities

Top 3

- ○ _____
- ○ _____
- ○ _____

Important Dates

Reminder

Health

- ○ _____
- ○ _____
- ○ _____
- ○ _____
- ○ _____

Finance

- ○ _____
- ○ _____
- ○ _____
- ○ _____
- ○ _____

Personal

- ○ _____
- ○ _____
- ○ _____
- ○ _____
- ○ _____

Career

- ○ _____
- ○ _____
- ○ _____
- ○ _____
- ○ _____

Habit Tracker

	1 2 3 4 5 6 7 8 9 10 11 12 13 14 15 16 17 18 19 20 21 22 23 24 25 26 27 28 29 30 31
_____	○○○○○○○○○○○○○○○○○○○○○○○○○○○○○○○
_____	○○○○○○○○○○○○○○○○○○○○○○○○○○○○○○○
_____	○○○○○○○○○○○○○○○○○○○○○○○○○○○○○○○
_____	○○○○○○○○○○○○○○○○○○○○○○○○○○○○○○○
_____	○○○○○○○○○○○○○○○○○○○○○○○○○○○○○○○

Weekly Priorities

Top 3 goals for the week

1. _____

2. _____

3. _____

To do list

- ☐ _____
- ☐ _____
- ☐ _____
- ☐ _____
- ☐ _____
- ☐ _____
- ☐ _____
- ☐ _____
- ☐ _____
- ☐ _____
- ☐ _____
- ☐ _____
- ☐ _____
- ☐ _____
- ☐ _____
- ☐ _____
- ☐ _____

Important	Positive Thoughts

ISAIAH 41:10

So do not fear, for I am with you; do not be dismayed, for I am your God. I will strengthen
you and help you; I will uphold you with my righteous right hand.

January 2022

27 Monday

28 Tuesday

29 Wednesday

30 Thursday

31 Friday

1 Saturday

2 Sunday

Weekly Priorities

Top 3 goals for the week

1. _____

2. _____

3. _____

To do list

- [ ] _____
- [ ] _____
- [ ] _____
- [ ] _____
- [ ] _____
- [ ] _____
- [ ] _____
- [ ] _____
- [ ] _____
- [ ] _____
- [ ] _____
- [ ] _____
- [ ] _____
- [ ] _____
- [ ] _____
- [ ] _____
- [ ] _____

Important	Positive Thoughts

January 2022

3 Monday

4 Tuesday

5 Wednesday

6 Thursday

7 Friday

8 Saturday

9 Sunday

Weekly Priorities

Top 3 goals for the week

1. _____
2. _____
3. _____

To do list

- [ ] _____
- [ ] _____
- [ ] _____
- [ ] _____
- [ ] _____
- [ ] _____
- [ ] _____
- [ ] _____
- [ ] _____
- [ ] _____
- [ ] _____
- [ ] _____
- [ ] _____
- [ ] _____
- [ ] _____
- [ ] _____
- [ ] _____
- [ ] _____

Important	Positive Thoughts

10 Monday

11 Tuesday

12 Wednesday

13 Thursday

14 Friday

15 Saturday

16 Sunday

Weekly Priorities

Top 3 goals for the week

1. _____

2. _____

3. _____

To do list

- [ ] _____
- [ ] _____
- [ ] _____
- [ ] _____
- [ ] _____
- [ ] _____
- [ ] _____
- [ ] _____
- [ ] _____
- [ ] _____
- [ ] _____
- [ ] _____
- [ ] _____
- [ ] _____
- [ ] _____
- [ ] _____
- [ ] _____

Important	Positive Thoughts

PROVERBS 18:21

The tongue has the power of life and death, and those who love it will eat its fruit.

17 Monday

18 Tuesday

19 Wednesday

20 Thursday

21 Friday

22 Saturday

23 Sunday

Weekly Priorities

Top 3 goals for the week

1. _____
2. _____
3. _____

To do list

- [ ] _____
- [ ] _____
- [ ] _____
- [ ] _____
- [ ] _____
- [ ] _____
- [ ] _____
- [ ] _____
- [ ] _____
- [ ] _____
- [ ] _____
- [ ] _____
- [ ] _____
- [ ] _____
- [ ] _____
- [ ] _____
- [ ] _____

Important	Positive Thoughts

24 Monday

25 Tuesday

26 Wednesday

27 Thursday

28 Friday

29 Saturday

30 Sunday

FEBRUARY 2022

Sunday	*Monday*	*Tuesday*	*Wednesday*
30	31	1	2 Groundhog Day
6	7	8	9
13	14 Valentine's Day	15 Presidents Day	16
20	21	22	23
27	28	1	2

FEBRUARY 2022

Thursday	Friday	Saturday	Notes
3	4	5	
10	11	12	
17	18	19	
24	25	26	
3	4	5	

JANUARY 2022

S	M	T	W	T	F	S
26	27	28	29	30	31	1
2	3	4	5	6	7	8
9	10	11	12	13	14	15
16	17	18	19	20	21	22
23	24	25	26	27	28	29
30	31					

MARCH 2022

S	M	T	W	T	F	S
27	28	1	2	3	4	5
6	7	8	9	10	11	12
13	14	15	16	17	18	19
20	21	22	23	24	25	26
27	28	29	30	31	1	2

Notes

Goals & Priorities

Top 3

- _____
- _____
- _____

Important Dates

Reminder

Health

- _____
- _____
- _____
- _____
- _____

Finance

- _____
- _____
- _____
- _____
- _____

Personal

- _____
- _____
- _____
- _____
- _____

Career

- _____
- _____
- _____
- _____
- _____

Habit Tracker

	1	2	3	4	5	6	7	8	9	10	11	12	13	14	15	16	17	18	19	20	21	22	23	24	25	26	27	28	29	30	31
_____	○	○	○	○	○	○	○	○	○	○	○	○	○	○	○	○	○	○	○	○	○	○	○	○	○	○	○	○	○	○	○
_____	○	○	○	○	○	○	○	○	○	○	○	○	○	○	○	○	○	○	○	○	○	○	○	○	○	○	○	○	○	○	○
_____	○	○	○	○	○	○	○	○	○	○	○	○	○	○	○	○	○	○	○	○	○	○	○	○	○	○	○	○	○	○	○
_____	○	○	○	○	○	○	○	○	○	○	○	○	○	○	○	○	○	○	○	○	○	○	○	○	○	○	○	○	○	○	○
_____	○	○	○	○	○	○	○	○	○	○	○	○	○	○	○	○	○	○	○	○	○	○	○	○	○	○	○	○	○	○	○

Weekly Priorities

Top 3 goals for the week

1. _____
2. _____
3. _____

To do list

- ☐ _____
- ☐ _____
- ☐ _____
- ☐ _____
- ☐ _____
- ☐ _____
- ☐ _____
- ☐ _____
- ☐ _____
- ☐ _____
- ☐ _____
- ☐ _____
- ☐ _____
- ☐ _____
- ☐ _____
- ☐ _____
- ☐ _____

Important	Positive Thoughts

February 2022

31 Monday

1 Tuesday

2 Wednesday

3 Thursday

4 Friday

5 Saturday

6 Sunday

Weekly Priorities

Top 3 goals for the week

1. _____

2. _____

3. _____

To do list

- [ ] _____
- [ ] _____
- [ ] _____
- [ ] _____
- [ ] _____
- [ ] _____
- [ ] _____
- [ ] _____
- [ ] _____
- [ ] _____
- [ ] _____
- [ ] _____
- [ ] _____
- [ ] _____
- [ ] _____
- [ ] _____
- [ ] _____
- [ ] _____

Important	Positive Thoughts

PSALMS 27:14

Wait for the Lord; be strong and take heart and wait for the Lord.

February 2022

7 Monday

8 Tuesday

9 Wednesday

10 Thursday

11 Friday

12 Saturday

13 Sunday

Weekly Priorities

Top 3 goals for the week

1. _____
2. _____
3. _____

To do list

- [ ] _____
- [ ] _____
- [ ] _____
- [ ] _____
- [ ] _____
- [ ] _____
- [ ] _____
- [ ] _____
- [ ] _____
- [ ] _____
- [ ] _____
- [ ] _____
- [ ] _____
- [ ] _____
- [ ] _____
- [ ] _____
- [ ] _____

Important	Positive Thoughts

EXODUS 14:14
"The LORD will fight for you; you need only to be still."

February 2022

14 Monday

15 Tuesday

16 Wednesday

17 Thursday

18 Friday

19 Saturday

20 Sunday

Weekly Priorities

Top 3 goals for the week

1. _____
2. _____
3. _____

To do list

- [ ] _____
- [ ] _____
- [ ] _____
- [ ] _____
- [ ] _____
- [ ] _____
- [ ] _____
- [ ] _____
- [ ] _____
- [ ] _____
- [ ] _____
- [ ] _____
- [ ] _____
- [ ] _____
- [ ] _____
- [ ] _____
- [ ] _____

Important	Positive Thoughts

Honor your father and your mother, so that you may live long in the land the LORD your God is giving you.

21 Monday

---

22 Tuesday

---

23 Wednesday

---

24 Thursday

---

25 Friday

---

26 Saturday

27 Sunday

MARCH 2022

Sunday	Monday	Tuesday	Wednesday
27	28	1	2
6	7	8	9
13 Daylight Savings Starts	14	15	16
20	21	22	23
27	28	29	30

MARCH 2022

Thursday	Friday	Saturday	Notes
3	4	5	
10	11	12	
17	18	19	
St. Patrick's Day			
24	25	26	
31	1	2	

FEBRUARY 2022

S	M	T	W	T	F	S
30	31	1	2	3	4	5
6	7	8	9	10	11	12
13	14	15	16	17	18	19
20	21	22	23	24	25	26
27	28	1	2	3	4	5

APRIL 2022

S	M	T	W	T	F	S
27	28	29	30	31	1	2
3	4	5	6	7	8	9
10	11	12	13	14	15	16
17	18	19	20	21	22	23
24	25	26	27	28	29	30

Notes

Goals & Priorities

Top 3

- ○ _____
- ○ _____
- ○ _____

Important Dates

Reminder

Health

- ○ _____
- ○ _____
- ○ _____
- ○ _____
- ○ _____

Finance

- ○ _____
- ○ _____
- ○ _____
- ○ _____
- ○ _____

Personal

- ○ _____
- ○ _____
- ○ _____
- ○ _____
- ○ _____

Career

- ○ _____
- ○ _____
- ○ _____
- ○ _____
- ○ _____

Habit Tracker

	1 2 3 4 5 6 7 8 9 10 11 12 13 14 15 16 17 18 19 20 21 22 23 24 25 26 27 28 29 30 31
_____	○○○○○○○○○○○○○○○○○○○○○○○○○○○○○○○
_____	○○○○○○○○○○○○○○○○○○○○○○○○○○○○○○○
_____	○○○○○○○○○○○○○○○○○○○○○○○○○○○○○○○
_____	○○○○○○○○○○○○○○○○○○○○○○○○○○○○○○○
_____	○○○○○○○○○○○○○○○○○○○○○○○○○○○○○○○

Weekly Priorities

Top 3 goals for the week

1. _____
2. _____
3. _____

To do list

- [ ] _____
- [ ] _____
- [ ] _____
- [ ] _____
- [ ] _____
- [ ] _____
- [ ] _____
- [ ] _____
- [ ] _____
- [ ] _____
- [ ] _____
- [ ] _____
- [ ] _____
- [ ] _____
- [ ] _____
- [ ] _____
- [ ] _____

Important	Positive Thoughts

ISAIAH 40:29

He gives strength to the weary and increases the power of the weak.

March 2022

28 Monday

1 Tuesday

2 Wednesday

3 Thursday

4 Friday

5 Saturday

6 Sunday

Weekly Priorities

Top 3 goals for the week

1. _____

2. _____

3. _____

To do list

- ☐ _____
- ☐ _____
- ☐ _____
- ☐ _____
- ☐ _____
- ☐ _____
- ☐ _____
- ☐ _____
- ☐ _____
- ☐ _____
- ☐ _____
- ☐ _____
- ☐ _____
- ☐ _____
- ☐ _____
- ☐ _____
- ☐ _____

Important	Positive Thoughts

ISAIAH 40:31

But those who hope in the LORD will renew their strength. They will soar on wings like
eagles; they will run and not grow weary, they will walk and not be faint.

March 2022

7 Monday

8 Tuesday

9 Wednesday

10 Thursday

11 Friday

12 Saturday

13 Sunday

Weekly Priorities

Top 3 goals for the week

1. _____
2. _____
3. _____

To do list

- [ ] _____
- [ ] _____
- [ ] _____
- [ ] _____
- [ ] _____
- [ ] _____
- [ ] _____
- [ ] _____
- [ ] _____
- [ ] _____
- [ ] _____
- [ ] _____
- [ ] _____
- [ ] _____
- [ ] _____
- [ ] _____
- [ ] _____

Important	Positive Thoughts

ISAIAH 41:13

For I am the LORD your God who takes hold of your right hand and says to you, Do not fear; I will help you.

14 Monday

15 Tuesday

16 Wednesday

17 Thursday

18 Friday

19 Saturday

20 Sunday

Weekly Priorities

Top 3 goals for the week

1. _____

2. _____

3. _____

To do list

- [ ] _____
- [ ] _____
- [ ] _____
- [ ] _____
- [ ] _____
- [ ] _____
- [ ] _____
- [ ] _____
- [ ] _____
- [ ] _____
- [ ] _____
- [ ] _____
- [ ] _____
- [ ] _____
- [ ] _____
- [ ] _____
- [ ] _____

Important	Positive Thoughts

ISAIAH 43:2

When you pass through the waters, I will be with you; and when you pass through the rivers, they will not sweep over you. When you walk through the fire, you will not be burned; the flames will not set you ablaze.

21 Monday

22 Tuesday

23 Wednesday

24 Thursday

25 Friday

26 Saturday

27 Sunday

APRIL 2022

Sunday	Monday	Tuesday	Wednesday
27	28	29	30
3	4	5	6
10	11	12	13
17	18	19	20
24	25	26	27

APRIL 2022

Thursday	Friday	Saturday	Notes
31	1	2	
7	8	9	
14	15 Good Friday	16	
21	22	23	
28	29	30	

MARCH 2022

S	M	T	W	T	F	S
27	28	1	2	3	4	5
6	7	8	9	10	11	12
13	14	15	16	17	18	19
20	21	22	23	24	25	26
27	28	29	30	31	1	2

MAY 2022

S	M	T	W	T	F	S
1	2	3	4	5	6	7
8	9	10	11	12	13	14
15	16	17	18	19	20	21
22	23	24	25	26	27	28
29	30	31	1	2	3	4

Notes

Goals & Priorities

Top 3

- ○ _____
- ○ _____
- ○ _____

Important Dates

Reminder

Health

- ○ _____
- ○ _____
- ○ _____
- ○ _____
- ○ _____

Finance

- ○ _____
- ○ _____
- ○ _____
- ○ _____
- ○ _____

Personal

- ○ _____
- ○ _____
- ○ _____
- ○ _____
- ○ _____

Career

- ○ _____
- ○ _____
- ○ _____
- ○ _____
- ○ _____

Habit Tracker

	1	2	3	4	5	6	7	8	9	10	11	12	13	14	15	16	17	18	19	20	21	22	23	24	25	26	27	28	29	30	31
_____	○	○	○	○	○	○	○	○	○	○	○	○	○	○	○	○	○	○	○	○	○	○	○	○	○	○	○	○	○	○	○
_____	○	○	○	○	○	○	○	○	○	○	○	○	○	○	○	○	○	○	○	○	○	○	○	○	○	○	○	○	○	○	○
_____	○	○	○	○	○	○	○	○	○	○	○	○	○	○	○	○	○	○	○	○	○	○	○	○	○	○	○	○	○	○	○
_____	○	○	○	○	○	○	○	○	○	○	○	○	○	○	○	○	○	○	○	○	○	○	○	○	○	○	○	○	○	○	○
_____	○	○	○	○	○	○	○	○	○	○	○	○	○	○	○	○	○	○	○	○	○	○	○	○	○	○	○	○	○	○	○

Weekly Priorities

Top 3 goals for the week

1. _____
2. _____
3. _____

To do list

- ☐ _____
- ☐ _____
- ☐ _____
- ☐ _____
- ☐ _____
- ☐ _____
- ☐ _____
- ☐ _____
- ☐ _____
- ☐ _____
- ☐ _____
- ☐ _____
- ☐ _____
- ☐ _____
- ☐ _____
- ☐ _____
- ☐ _____
- ☐ _____

Important	Positive Thoughts

ISAIAH 54:10

Though the mountains be shaken and the hills be removed, yet my unfailing love for you will not be shaken

nor my covenant of peace be removed," says the LORD, who has compassion on you.

April 2022

28 Monday

29 Tuesday

30 Wednesday

31 Thursday

1 Friday

2 Saturday

3 Sunday

Weekly Priorities

Top 3 goals for the week

1. _____
2. _____
3. _____

To do list

- [ ] _____
- [ ] _____
- [ ] _____
- [ ] _____
- [ ] _____
- [ ] _____
- [ ] _____
- [ ] _____
- [ ] _____
- [ ] _____
- [ ] _____
- [ ] _____
- [ ] _____
- [ ] _____
- [ ] _____
- [ ] _____

Important	Positive Thoughts

April 2022

4 Monday

5 Tuesday

6 Wednesday

7 Thursday

8 Friday

9 Saturday

10 Sunday

Weekly Priorities

Top 3 goals for the week

1. _____

2. _____

3. _____

To do list

- [ ] _____
- [ ] _____
- [ ] _____
- [ ] _____
- [ ] _____
- [ ] _____
- [ ] _____
- [ ] _____
- [ ] _____
- [ ] _____
- [ ] _____
- [ ] _____
- [ ] _____
- [ ] _____
- [ ] _____
- [ ] _____
- [ ] _____

Important	Positive Thoughts

ISAIAH 58:6

Is not this the kind of fasting I have chosen: to loose the chains of injustice and untie the
cords of the yoke, to set the oppressed free and break every yoke?

11 Monday

12 Tuesday

13 Wednesday

14 Thursday

15 Friday

16 Saturday

17 Sunday

Weekly Priorities

Top 3 goals for the week

1. _____
2. _____
3. _____

To do list

- [ ] _____
- [ ] _____
- [ ] _____
- [ ] _____
- [ ] _____
- [ ] _____
- [ ] _____
- [ ] _____
- [ ] _____
- [ ] _____
- [ ] _____
- [ ] _____
- [ ] _____
- [ ] _____
- [ ] _____
- [ ] _____

Important	Positive Thoughts

ISAIAH 61:1

The Spirit of the Sovereign LORD is on me, because the LORD has anointed me to proclaim good news to the poor. He has sent me to bind up the brokenhearted, to proclaim freedom for the captives and release from darkness for the prisoners,

18 Monday

19 Tuesday

20 Wednesday

21 Thursday

22 Friday

23 Saturday

24 Sunday

Weekly Priorities

Top 3 goals for the week

1. _____
2. _____
3. _____

To do list

- [ ] _____
- [ ] _____
- [ ] _____
- [ ] _____
- [ ] _____
- [ ] _____
- [ ] _____
- [ ] _____
- [ ] _____
- [ ] _____
- [ ] _____
- [ ] _____
- [ ] _____
- [ ] _____
- [ ] _____
- [ ] _____
- [ ] _____

Important	Positive Thoughts

JAMES 1:5

If any of you lacks wisdom, you should ask God, who gives generously to all without finding fault, and it will be given to you.

25 Monday

26 Tuesday

27 Wednesday

28 Thursday

29 Friday

30 Saturday

1 Sunday

MAY 2022

Sunday	Monday	Tuesday	Wednesday
1	2	3	4
8	9 Mother's Day	10	11
15	16	17	18
22	23	24	25
29	30 Memorial Day	31	1

MAY 2022

Thursday	Friday	Saturday	Notes
5	6	7	
12	13	14	
19	20	21 Armed Forces Day	
26	27	28	
2	3	4	

APRIL 2022

S	M	T	W	T	F	S
27	28	29	30	31	1	2
3	4	5	6	7	8	9
10	11	12	13	14	15	16
17	18	19	20	21	22	23
24	25	26	27	28	29	30

JUNE 2022

S	M	T	W	T	F	S
29	30	31	1	2	3	4
5	6	7	8	9	10	11
12	13	14	15	16	17	18
19	20	21	22	23	24	25
26	27	28	29	30	1	2

Notes

Goals & Priorities

Top 3

- ○ _____
- ○ _____
- ○ _____

Important Dates

Reminder

Health

- ○ _____
- ○ _____
- ○ _____
- ○ _____
- ○ _____

Finance

- ○ _____
- ○ _____
- ○ _____
- ○ _____
- ○ _____

Personal

- ○ _____
- ○ _____
- ○ _____
- ○ _____
- ○ _____

Career

- ○ _____
- ○ _____
- ○ _____
- ○ _____
- ○ _____

Habit Tracker

	1	2	3	4	5	6	7	8	9	10	11	12	13	14	15	16	17	18	19	20	21	22	23	24	25	26	27	28	29	30	31
_____	○	○	○	○	○	○	○	○	○	○	○	○	○	○	○	○	○	○	○	○	○	○	○	○	○	○	○	○	○	○	○
_____	○	○	○	○	○	○	○	○	○	○	○	○	○	○	○	○	○	○	○	○	○	○	○	○	○	○	○	○	○	○	○
_____	○	○	○	○	○	○	○	○	○	○	○	○	○	○	○	○	○	○	○	○	○	○	○	○	○	○	○	○	○	○	○
_____	○	○	○	○	○	○	○	○	○	○	○	○	○	○	○	○	○	○	○	○	○	○	○	○	○	○	○	○	○	○	○
_____	○	○	○	○	○	○	○	○	○	○	○	○	○	○	○	○	○	○	○	○	○	○	○	○	○	○	○	○	○	○	○

Weekly Priorities

Top 3 goals for the week

1. _____
2. _____
3. _____

To do list

- [ ] _____
- [ ] _____
- [ ] _____
- [ ] _____
- [ ] _____
- [ ] _____
- [ ] _____
- [ ] _____
- [ ] _____
- [ ] _____
- [ ] _____
- [ ] _____
- [ ] _____
- [ ] _____
- [ ] _____
- [ ] _____

Important	Positive Thoughts

JAMES 4:7

Submit yourselves, then, to God. Resist the devil, and he will flee from you.

2 Monday

---

3 Tuesday

---

4 Wednesday

---

5 Thursday

---

6 Friday

---

7 Saturday

8 Sunday

Weekly Priorities

Top 3 goals for the week

1. _____

2. _____

3. _____

To do list

- ☐ _____
- ☐ _____
- ☐ _____
- ☐ _____
- ☐ _____
- ☐ _____
- ☐ _____
- ☐ _____
- ☐ _____
- ☐ _____
- ☐ _____
- ☐ _____
- ☐ _____
- ☐ _____
- ☐ _____
- ☐ _____
- ☐ _____

Important	Positive Thoughts

May 2022

9 Monday

10 Tuesday

11 Wednesday

12 Thursday

13 Friday

14 Saturday

15 Sunday

Weekly Priorities

Top 3 goals for the week

1. _____
2. _____
3. _____

To do list

- [ ]
- [ ]
- [ ]
- [ ]
- [ ]
- [ ]
- [ ]
- [ ]
- [ ]
- [ ]
- [ ]
- [ ]
- [ ]
- [ ]
- [ ]
- [ ]

Important

Positive Thoughts

2 CHRONICLES 7:14

If my people, who are called by my name, will humble themselves and pray and seek my face and turn from their wicked ways, then I will hear from heaven, and I will forgive their sin and will heal their land.

16 Monday

17 Tuesday

18 Wednesday

19 Thursday

20 Friday

21 Saturday

22 Sunday

Weekly Priorities

Top 3 goals for the week

1. _____
2. _____
3. _____

To do list

- [ ]
- [ ]
- [ ]
- [ ]
- [ ]
- [ ]
- [ ]
- [ ]
- [ ]
- [ ]
- [ ]
- [ ]
- [ ]
- [ ]
- [ ]
- [ ]
- [ ]

Important	Positive Thoughts

DEUTERONOMY 31:8

The LORD himself goes before you and will be with you; he will never leave you nor forsake you. Do not be afraid; do not be discouraged.

23 Monday

24 Tuesday

25 Wednesday

26 Thursday

27 Friday

28 Saturday

29 Sunday

JUNE 2022

Sunday	Monday	Tuesday	Wednesday
29	30	31	1
5	6	7	8
12	13	14 Flag Day	15
19 Father's Day	20	21	22
26	27	28	29

JUNE 2022

Thursday	Friday	Saturday	Notes
2	3	4	
9	10	11	
16	17	18	
23	24	25	
30	1	2	

MAY 2022

S	M	T	W	T	F	S
1	2	3	4	5	6	7
8	9	10	11	12	13	14
15	16	17	18	19	20	21
22	23	24	25	26	27	28
29	30	31	1	2	3	4

JULY 2022

S	M	T	W	T	F	S
26	27	28	29	30	1	2
3	4	5	6	7	8	9
10	11	12	13	14	15	16
17	18	19	20	21	22	23
24	25	26	27	28	29	30
31						

Notes

Goals & Priorities

Top 3

- ○ _____
- ○ _____
- ○ _____

Important Dates

Reminder

Health

- ○ _____
- ○ _____
- ○ _____
- ○ _____
- ○ _____

Finance

- ○ _____
- ○ _____
- ○ _____
- ○ _____
- ○ _____

Personal

- ○ _____
- ○ _____
- ○ _____
- ○ _____
- ○ _____

Career

- ○ _____
- ○ _____
- ○ _____
- ○ _____
- ○ _____

Habit Tracker

1	2	3	4	5	6	7	8	9	10	11	12	13	14	15	16	17	18	19	20	21	22	23	24	25	26	27	28	29	30	31
○	○	○	○	○	○	○	○	○	○	○	○	○	○	○	○	○	○	○	○	○	○	○	○	○	○	○	○	○	○	○
○	○	○	○	○	○	○	○	○	○	○	○	○	○	○	○	○	○	○	○	○	○	○	○	○	○	○	○	○	○	○
○	○	○	○	○	○	○	○	○	○	○	○	○	○	○	○	○	○	○	○	○	○	○	○	○	○	○	○	○	○	○
○	○	○	○	○	○	○	○	○	○	○	○	○	○	○	○	○	○	○	○	○	○	○	○	○	○	○	○	○	○	○
○	○	○	○	○	○	○	○	○	○	○	○	○	○	○	○	○	○	○	○	○	○	○	○	○	○	○	○	○	○	○

Weekly Priorities

Top 3 goals for the week

1. _____
2. _____
3. _____

To do list

- ☐ _____
- ☐ _____
- ☐ _____
- ☐ _____
- ☐ _____
- ☐ _____
- ☐ _____
- ☐ _____
- ☐ _____
- ☐ _____
- ☐ _____
- ☐ _____
- ☐ _____
- ☐ _____
- ☐ _____
- ☐ _____
- ☐ _____

Important	Positive Thoughts

30 Monday

31 Tuesday

1 Wednesday

2 Thursday

3 Friday

4 Saturday

5 Sunday

Weekly Priorities

Top 3 goals for the week

1. _____

2. _____

3. _____

To do list

- ☐ _____
- ☐ _____
- ☐ _____
- ☐ _____
- ☐ _____
- ☐ _____
- ☐ _____
- ☐ _____
- ☐ _____
- ☐ _____
- ☐ _____
- ☐ _____
- ☐ _____
- ☐ _____
- ☐ _____
- ☐ _____
- ☐ _____

Important	Positive Thoughts

6 Monday

7 Tuesday

8 Wednesday

9 Thursday

10 Friday

11 Saturday

12 Sunday

Weekly Priorities

Top 3 goals for the week

1. _____
2. _____
3. _____

To do list

- [ ] _____
- [ ] _____
- [ ] _____
- [ ] _____
- [ ] _____
- [ ] _____
- [ ] _____
- [ ] _____
- [ ] _____
- [ ] _____
- [ ] _____
- [ ] _____
- [ ] _____
- [ ] _____
- [ ] _____
- [ ] _____
- [ ] _____

Important

Positive Thoughts

13 Monday

---

14 Tuesday

---

15 Wednesday

---

16 Thursday

---

17 Friday

---

18 Saturday

19 Sunday

Weekly Priorities

Top 3 goals for the week

1. _____
2. _____
3. _____

To do list

- ☐ _____
- ☐ _____
- ☐ _____
- ☐ _____
- ☐ _____
- ☐ _____
- ☐ _____
- ☐ _____
- ☐ _____
- ☐ _____
- ☐ _____
- ☐ _____
- ☐ _____
- ☐ _____
- ☐ _____
- ☐ _____
- ☐ _____

Important	Positive Thoughts

20 Monday

21 Tuesday

22 Wednesday

23 Thursday

24 Friday

25 Saturday

26 Sunday

Weekly Priorities

Top 3 goals for the week

1. _____
2. _____
3. _____

To do list

- [ ] _____
- [ ] _____
- [ ] _____
- [ ] _____
- [ ] _____
- [ ] _____
- [ ] _____
- [ ] _____
- [ ] _____
- [ ] _____
- [ ] _____
- [ ] _____
- [ ] _____
- [ ] _____
- [ ] _____
- [ ] _____
- [ ] _____
- [ ] _____

Important	Positive Thoughts

MALACHI 3:10

Bring the whole tithe into the storehouse, that there may be food in my house. Test me in this, says the LORD Almighty, and see if I will not throw open the floodgates of heaven and pour out so much blessing that there will not be room enough to store it.

27 Monday

28 Tuesday

29 Wednesday

30 Thursday

1 Friday

2 Saturday

3 Sunday

JULY 2022

Sunday	Monday	Tuesday	Wednesday
26	27	28	29
3	4 Independence Day	5	6
10	11	12	13
17	18	19	20
24 31 Parents' Day	25	26	27

JULY 2022

Thursday	*Friday*	*Saturday*	*Notes*
30	1	2	
7	8	9	
14	15	16	
21	22	23	
28	29	30	

JUNE 2022

S	M	T	W	T	F	S
29	30	31	1	2	3	4
5	6	7	8	9	10	11
12	13	14	15	16	17	18
19	20	21	22	23	24	25
26	27	28	29	30	1	2

AUGUST 2022

S	M	T	W	T	F	S
31	1	2	3	4	5	6
7	8	9	10	11	12	13
14	15	16	17	18	19	20
21	22	23	24	25	26	27
28	29	30	31	1	2	3

Notes

Goals & Priorities

Top 3

○ _____

○ _____

○ _____

Important Dates

Reminder

Health

○ _____
○ _____
○ _____
○ _____
○ _____

Finance

○ _____
○ _____
○ _____
○ _____
○ _____

Personal

○ _____
○ _____
○ _____
○ _____
○ _____

Career

○ _____
○ _____
○ _____
○ _____
○ _____

Habit Tracker

	1	2	3	4	5	6	7	8	9	10	11	12	13	14	15	16	17	18	19	20	21	22	23	24	25	26	27	28	29	30	31
_____	○	○	○	○	○	○	○	○	○	○	○	○	○	○	○	○	○	○	○	○	○	○	○	○	○	○	○	○	○	○	○
_____	○	○	○	○	○	○	○	○	○	○	○	○	○	○	○	○	○	○	○	○	○	○	○	○	○	○	○	○	○	○	○
_____	○	○	○	○	○	○	○	○	○	○	○	○	○	○	○	○	○	○	○	○	○	○	○	○	○	○	○	○	○	○	○
_____	○	○	○	○	○	○	○	○	○	○	○	○	○	○	○	○	○	○	○	○	○	○	○	○	○	○	○	○	○	○	○
_____	○	○	○	○	○	○	○	○	○	○	○	○	○	○	○	○	○	○	○	○	○	○	○	○	○	○	○	○	○	○	○

Weekly Priorities

Top 3 goals for the week

1. _____
2. _____
3. _____

To do list

- [ ]
- [ ]
- [ ]
- [ ]
- [ ]
- [ ]
- [ ]
- [ ]
- [ ]
- [ ]
- [ ]
- [ ]
- [ ]
- [ ]
- [ ]
- [ ]
- [ ]

Important	Positive Thoughts

MARK 11:24

Therefore I tell you, whatever you ask for in prayer, believe that you have received it, and it will be yours.

4 Monday

5 Tuesday

6 Wednesday

7 Thursday

8 Friday

9 Saturday

10 Sunday

Weekly Priorities

Top 3 goals for the week

1. _____

2. _____

3. _____

To do list

☐ _____
☐ _____
☐ _____
☐ _____
☐ _____
☐ _____
☐ _____
☐ _____
☐ _____
☐ _____
☐ _____
☐ _____
☐ _____
☐ _____
☐ _____
☐ _____
☐ _____
☐ _____

Important	Positive Thoughts

JOSHUA 1:9

Have I not commanded you? Be strong and courageous. Do not be afraid; do not be
discouraged, for the LORD your God will be with you wherever you go.

July 2022

11 Monday

12 Tuesday

13 Wednesday

14 Thursday

15 Friday

16 Saturday

17 Sunday

Weekly Priorities

Top 3 goals for the week

1. _____

2. _____

3. _____

To do list

- [ ] _____
- [ ] _____
- [ ] _____
- [ ] _____
- [ ] _____
- [ ] _____
- [ ] _____
- [ ] _____
- [ ] _____
- [ ] _____
- [ ] _____
- [ ] _____
- [ ] _____
- [ ] _____
- [ ] _____
- [ ] _____
- [ ] _____

Important	Positive Thoughts

PHILIPPIANS 4:19

And my God will meet all your needs according to the riches of his glory in Christ Jesus.

18 Monday

19 Tuesday

20 Wednesday

21 Thursday

22 Friday

23 Saturday

24 Sunday

Weekly Priorities

Top 3 goals for the week

1. _____
2. _____
3. _____

To do list

- ☐ _____
- ☐ _____
- ☐ _____
- ☐ _____
- ☐ _____
- ☐ _____
- ☐ _____
- ☐ _____
- ☐ _____
- ☐ _____
- ☐ _____
- ☐ _____
- ☐ _____
- ☐ _____
- ☐ _____
- ☐ _____
- ☐ _____
- ☐ _____

Important	Positive Thoughts

25 Monday

26 Tuesday

27 Wednesday

28 Thursday

29 Friday

30 Saturday

31 Sunday

AUGUST 2022

Sunday	Monday	Tuesday	Wednesday
31	1	2	3
7	8	9	10
14	15	16	17
21	22	23	24
28	29	30	31

AUGUST 2022

Thursday	*Friday*	*Saturday*	*Notes*
4	5	6	
11	12	13	
18	19	20	
25	26	27	
1	2	3	

JULY 2022

S	M	T	W	T	F	S
26	27	28	29	30	1	2
3	4	5	6	7	8	9
10	11	12	13	14	15	16
17	18	19	20	21	22	23
24	25	26	27	28	29	30

SEPTEMBER 2022

S	M	T	W	T	F	S
28	29	30	31	1	2	3
4	5	6	7	8	9	10
11	12	13	14	15	16	17
18	19	20	21	22	23	24
25	26	27	28	29	30	1

Notes

Goals & Priorities

Top 3

- ○
- ○
- ○

Important Dates

Reminder

Health

- ○
- ○
- ○
- ○
- ○

Finance

- ○
- ○
- ○
- ○
- ○

Personal

- ○
- ○
- ○
- ○
- ○

Career

- ○
- ○
- ○
- ○
- ○

Habit Tracker

	1	2	3	4	5	6	7	8	9	10	11	12	13	14	15	16	17	18	19	20	21	22	23	24	25	26	27	28	29	30	31
	○	○	○	○	○	○	○	○	○	○	○	○	○	○	○	○	○	○	○	○	○	○	○	○	○	○	○	○	○	○	○
	○	○	○	○	○	○	○	○	○	○	○	○	○	○	○	○	○	○	○	○	○	○	○	○	○	○	○	○	○	○	○
	○	○	○	○	○	○	○	○	○	○	○	○	○	○	○	○	○	○	○	○	○	○	○	○	○	○	○	○	○	○	○
	○	○	○	○	○	○	○	○	○	○	○	○	○	○	○	○	○	○	○	○	○	○	○	○	○	○	○	○	○	○	○
	○	○	○	○	○	○	○	○	○	○	○	○	○	○	○	○	○	○	○	○	○	○	○	○	○	○	○	○	○	○	○

Weekly Priorities

Top 3 goals for the week

1. _____
2. _____
3. _____

To do list

☐ _____
☐ _____
☐ _____
☐ _____
☐ _____
☐ _____
☐ _____
☐ _____
☐ _____
☐ _____
☐ _____
☐ _____
☐ _____
☐ _____
☐ _____
☐ _____
☐ _____

Important	Positive Thoughts

August 2022

1 Monday

2 Tuesday

3 Wednesday

4 Thursday

5 Friday

6 Saturday

7 Sunday

Weekly Priorities

Top 3 goals for the week

1. _____
2. _____
3. _____

To do list

- ☐ _____
- ☐ _____
- ☐ _____
- ☐ _____
- ☐ _____
- ☐ _____
- ☐ _____
- ☐ _____
- ☐ _____
- ☐ _____
- ☐ _____
- ☐ _____
- ☐ _____
- ☐ _____
- ☐ _____
- ☐ _____
- ☐ _____

Important	Positive Thoughts

PSALM 27:1

The LORD is my light and my salvation— whom shall I fear? The LORD is the stronghold of my life— of whom shall I be afraid?

August 2022

8 Monday

9 Tuesday

10 Wednesday

11 Thursday

12 Friday

13 Saturday

14 Sunday

Weekly Priorities

Top 3 goals for the week

1. _____
2. _____
3. _____

To do list

- [ ] _____
- [ ] _____
- [ ] _____
- [ ] _____
- [ ] _____
- [ ] _____
- [ ] _____
- [ ] _____
- [ ] _____
- [ ] _____
- [ ] _____
- [ ] _____
- [ ] _____
- [ ] _____
- [ ] _____
- [ ] _____
- [ ] _____

Important

Positive Thoughts

PSALM 34:17

The righteous cry out, and the LORD hears them; he delivers them from all their troubles.

August 2022

15 Monday

16 Tuesday

17 Wednesday

18 Thursday

19 Friday

20 Saturday

21 Sunday

Weekly Priorities

Top 3 goals for the week

1. _____

2. _____

3. _____

To do list

☐ _____
☐ _____
☐ _____
☐ _____
☐ _____
☐ _____
☐ _____
☐ _____
☐ _____
☐ _____
☐ _____
☐ _____
☐ _____
☐ _____
☐ _____
☐ _____
☐ _____

Important	Positive Thoughts

PSALM 37:4
Take delight in the LORD, and he will give you the desires of your heart.

22 Monday

23 Tuesday

24 Wednesday

25 Thursday

26 Friday

27 Saturday

28 Sunday

SEPTEMBER 2022

Sunday	Monday	Tuesday	Wednesday
28	29	30	31
4	5 Labor Day	6	7
11 Grandparents' Day	12	13	14
18	19	20	21
25	26	27	28

SEPTEMBER 2022

Thursday	*Friday*	*Saturday*	*Notes*
1	2	3	_____
8	9	10	_____
15	16	17	_____
22	23	24	
29	30	1	

AUGUST 2022

S	M	T	W	T	F	S
31	1	2	3	4	5	6
7	8	9	10	11	12	13
14	15	16	17	18	19	20
21	22	23	24	25	26	27
28	29	30	31	1	2	3

OCTOBER 2022

S	M	T	W	T	F	S
25	26	27	28	29	30	1
2	3	4	5	6	7	8
9	10	11	12	13	14	15
16	17	18	19	20	21	22
23	24	25	26	27	28	29
30	31					

Notes

Goals & Priorities

Top 3

○
○
○

Important Dates

Reminder

Health

○
○
○
○
○

Finance

○
○
○
○
○

Personal

○
○
○
○
○

Career

○
○
○
○
○

Habit Tracker

1 2 3 4 5 6 7 8 9 10 11 12 13 14 15 16 17 18 19 20 21 22 23 24 25 26 27 28 29 30 31

○○○○○○○○○○○○○○○○○○○○○○○○○○○○○○○

○○○○○○○○○○○○○○○○○○○○○○○○○○○○○○○

○○○○○○○○○○○○○○○○○○○○○○○○○○○○○○○

○○○○○○○○○○○○○○○○○○○○○○○○○○○○○○○

○○○○○○○○○○○○○○○○○○○○○○○○○○○○○○○

Weekly Priorities

Top 3 goals for the week

1. _____

2. _____

3. _____

To do list

- ☐ _____
- ☐ _____
- ☐ _____
- ☐ _____
- ☐ _____
- ☐ _____
- ☐ _____
- ☐ _____
- ☐ _____
- ☐ _____
- ☐ _____
- ☐ _____
- ☐ _____
- ☐ _____
- ☐ _____
- ☐ _____
- ☐ _____

Important	Positive Thoughts

PSALM 50:15

And call on me in the day of trouble; I will deliver you, and you will honor me.

29 Monday

30 Tuesday

31 Wednesday

1 Thursday

2 Friday

3 Saturday

4 Sunday

Weekly Priorities

Top 3 goals for the week

1. _____
2. _____
3. _____

To do list

- [ ] _____
- [ ] _____
- [ ] _____
- [ ] _____
- [ ] _____
- [ ] _____
- [ ] _____
- [ ] _____
- [ ] _____
- [ ] _____
- [ ] _____
- [ ] _____
- [ ] _____
- [ ] _____
- [ ] _____
- [ ] _____
- [ ] _____

Important	Positive Thoughts

5 Monday

6 Tuesday

7 Wednesday

8 Thursday

9 Friday

10 Saturday

11 Sunday

Weekly Priorities

Top 3 goals for the week

1. _____

2. _____

3. _____

To do list

- [ ] _____
- [ ] _____
- [ ] _____
- [ ] _____
- [ ] _____
- [ ] _____
- [ ] _____
- [ ] _____
- [ ] _____
- [ ] _____
- [ ] _____
- [ ] _____
- [ ] _____
- [ ] _____
- [ ] _____
- [ ] _____
- [ ] _____

Important	Positive Thoughts

PROVERBS 13:11

Dishonest money dwindles away, but whoever gathers money little by little makes it grow.

12 Monday

13 Tuesday

14 Wednesday

15 Thursday

16 Friday

17 Saturday

18 Sunday

Weekly Priorities

Top 3 goals for the week

1. _____

2. _____

3. _____

To do list

- [ ] _____
- [ ] _____
- [ ] _____
- [ ] _____
- [ ] _____
- [ ] _____
- [ ] _____
- [ ] _____
- [ ] _____
- [ ] _____
- [ ] _____
- [ ] _____
- [ ] _____
- [ ] _____
- [ ] _____
- [ ] _____
- [ ] _____

Important	Positive Thoughts

PROVERBS 22:6

Start children off on the way they should go, and even when they are old they will not turn from it.

19 Monday

20 Tuesday

21 Wednesday

22 Thursday

23 Friday

24 Saturday

25 Sunday

Weekly Priorities

Top 3 goals for the week

1. _____

2. _____

3. _____

To do list

- [ ] _____
- [ ] _____
- [ ] _____
- [ ] _____
- [ ] _____
- [ ] _____
- [ ] _____
- [ ] _____
- [ ] _____
- [ ] _____
- [ ] _____
- [ ] _____
- [ ] _____
- [ ] _____
- [ ] _____
- [ ] _____
- [ ] _____

Important	Positive Thoughts

REVELATION 3:5

The one who is victorious will, like them, be dressed in white. I will never blot out the name of that person

from the book of life, but will acknowledge that name before my Father and his angels.

26 Monday

27 Tuesday

28 Wednesday

29 Thursday

30 Friday

1 Saturday

2 Sunday

OCTOBER 2022

Sunday	Monday	Tuesday	Wednesday
25	26	27	28
2	3	4	5
9	10 Columbus Day	11	12
16	17	18	19
23	24	25	26
30	31 Halloween		

OCTOBER 2022

Thursday	*Friday*	*Saturday*	*Notes*
29	30	1	
6	7	8	
13	14	15	
20	21	22	
27	28	29	

SEPTEMBER 2022

S	M	T	W	T	F	S
28	29	30	31	1	2	3
4	5	6	7	8	9	10
11	12	13	14	15	16	17
18	19	20	21	22	23	24
25	26	27	28	29	30	1

NOVEMBER 2022

S	M	T	W	T	F	S
30	31	1	2	3	4	5
6	7	8	9	10	11	12
13	14	15	16	17	18	19
20	21	22	23	24	25	26
27	28	29	30	1	2	3

Notes

Goals & Priorities

Top 3

○ _____

○ _____

○ _____

Important Dates

Reminder

Health

○ _____

○ _____

○ _____

○ _____

○ _____

Finance

○ _____

○ _____

○ _____

○ _____

○ _____

Personal

○ _____

○ _____

○ _____

○ _____

○ _____

Career

○ _____

○ _____

○ _____

○ _____

○ _____

Habit Tracker

	1	2	3	4	5	6	7	8	9	10	11	12	13	14	15	16	17	18	19	20	21	22	23	24	25	26	27	28	29	30	31
_____	○	○	○	○	○	○	○	○	○	○	○	○	○	○	○	○	○	○	○	○	○	○	○	○	○	○	○	○	○	○	○
_____	○	○	○	○	○	○	○	○	○	○	○	○	○	○	○	○	○	○	○	○	○	○	○	○	○	○	○	○	○	○	○
_____	○	○	○	○	○	○	○	○	○	○	○	○	○	○	○	○	○	○	○	○	○	○	○	○	○	○	○	○	○	○	○
_____	○	○	○	○	○	○	○	○	○	○	○	○	○	○	○	○	○	○	○	○	○	○	○	○	○	○	○	○	○	○	○
_____	○	○	○	○	○	○	○	○	○	○	○	○	○	○	○	○	○	○	○	○	○	○	○	○	○	○	○	○	○	○	○

Weekly Priorities

Top 3 goals for the week

1. _____

2. _____

3. _____

To do list

- [ ]
- [ ]
- [ ]
- [ ]
- [ ]
- [ ]
- [ ]
- [ ]
- [ ]
- [ ]
- [ ]
- [ ]
- [ ]
- [ ]
- [ ]
- [ ]
- [ ]

Important	Positive Thoughts

3 Monday

4 Tuesday

5 Wednesday

6 Thursday

7 Friday

8 Saturday

9 Sunday

Weekly Priorities

Top 3 goals for the week

1. _____
2. _____
3. _____

To do list

- [ ] _____
- [ ] _____
- [ ] _____
- [ ] _____
- [ ] _____
- [ ] _____
- [ ] _____
- [ ] _____
- [ ] _____
- [ ] _____
- [ ] _____
- [ ] _____
- [ ] _____
- [ ] _____
- [ ] _____
- [ ] _____
- [ ] _____

Important	Positive Thoughts

October 2022

10 Monday

11 Tuesday

12 Wednesday

13 Thursday

14 Friday

15 Saturday

16 Sunday

Weekly Priorities

Top 3 goals for the week

1. _____
2. _____
3. _____

To do list

- ☐ _____
- ☐ _____
- ☐ _____
- ☐ _____
- ☐ _____
- ☐ _____
- ☐ _____
- ☐ _____
- ☐ _____
- ☐ _____
- ☐ _____
- ☐ _____
- ☐ _____
- ☐ _____
- ☐ _____
- ☐ _____
- ☐ _____
- ☐ _____

Important	Positive Thoughts

PSALM 9:9-10

The LORD is a refuge for the oppressed, a stronghold in times of trouble. Those who know your
name trust in you, for you, LORD, have never forsaken those who seek you.

17 Monday

18 Tuesday

19 Wednesday

20 Thursday

21 Friday

22 Saturday

23 Sunday

Weekly Priorities

Top 3 goals for the week

1. _____
2. _____
3. _____

To do list

- [ ] _____
- [ ] _____
- [ ] _____
- [ ] _____
- [ ] _____
- [ ] _____
- [ ] _____
- [ ] _____
- [ ] _____
- [ ] _____
- [ ] _____
- [ ] _____
- [ ] _____
- [ ] _____
- [ ] _____
- [ ] _____
- [ ] _____

Important	Positive Thoughts

PHILIPPIANS 4:6-7

Do not be anxious about anything, but in every situation, by prayer and petition, with thanksgiving, present your requests to God. And the peace of God, which transcends all understanding, will guard your hearts and your minds in Christ Jesus.

24 Monday

25 Tuesday

26 Wednesday

27 Thursday

28 Friday

29 Saturday

30 Sunday

NOVEMBER 2022

Sunday	Monday	Tuesday	Wednesday
30	31	1	2
6 Daylight Saving Time Ends	7	8	9
13	14	15	16
20	21	22	23
27	28 Cyber Monday	29	30

NOVEMBER 2022

Thursday	Friday	Saturday	Notes
3	4	5	
10	11	12	
	Veteran's Day		
17	18	19	
24	25	26	
Thanksgiving	Black Friday		
1	2	3	

OCTOBER 2022

S	M	T	W	T	F	S
25	26	27	28	29	30	1
2	3	4	5	6	7	8
9	10	11	12	13	14	15
16	17	18	19	20	21	22
23	24	25	26	27	28	29
30	31					

DECEMBER 2022

S	M	T	W	T	F	S
27	28	29	30	1	2	3
4	5	6	7	8	9	10
11	12	13	14	15	16	17
18	19	20	21	22	23	24
25	26	27	28	29	30	31

Notes

Goals & Priorities

Top 3

- _____
- _____
- _____

Important Dates

Reminder

Health

- ○ _____
- ○ _____
- ○ _____
- ○ _____
- ○ _____

Finance

- ○ _____
- ○ _____
- ○ _____
- ○ _____
- ○ _____

Personal

- ○ _____
- ○ _____
- ○ _____
- ○ _____
- ○ _____

Career

- ○ _____
- ○ _____
- ○ _____
- ○ _____
- ○ _____

Habit Tracker

	1	2	3	4	5	6	7	8	9	10	11	12	13	14	15	16	17	18	19	20	21	22	23	24	25	26	27	28	29	30	31
_____	○	○	○	○	○	○	○	○	○	○	○	○	○	○	○	○	○	○	○	○	○	○	○	○	○	○	○	○	○	○	○
_____	○	○	○	○	○	○	○	○	○	○	○	○	○	○	○	○	○	○	○	○	○	○	○	○	○	○	○	○	○	○	○
_____	○	○	○	○	○	○	○	○	○	○	○	○	○	○	○	○	○	○	○	○	○	○	○	○	○	○	○	○	○	○	○
_____	○	○	○	○	○	○	○	○	○	○	○	○	○	○	○	○	○	○	○	○	○	○	○	○	○	○	○	○	○	○	○
_____	○	○	○	○	○	○	○	○	○	○	○	○	○	○	○	○	○	○	○	○	○	○	○	○	○	○	○	○	○	○	○

Weekly Priorities

Top 3 goals for the week

1. _____
2. _____
3. _____

To do list

- [ ] _____
- [ ] _____
- [ ] _____
- [ ] _____
- [ ] _____
- [ ] _____
- [ ] _____
- [ ] _____
- [ ] _____
- [ ] _____
- [ ] _____
- [ ] _____
- [ ] _____
- [ ] _____
- [ ] _____
- [ ] _____
- [ ] _____

Important	Positive Thoughts

PROVERBS 3:5-6

Trust in the LORD with all your heart and lean not on your own understanding; in all

your ways submit to him, and he will make your paths straight.

November 2022

31 Monday

1 Tuesday

2 Wednesday

3 Thursday

4 Friday

5 Saturday

6 Sunday

Weekly Priorities

Top 3 goals for the week

1. _____
2. _____
3. _____

To do list

- [ ] _____
- [ ] _____
- [ ] _____
- [ ] _____
- [ ] _____
- [ ] _____
- [ ] _____
- [ ] _____
- [ ] _____
- [ ] _____
- [ ] _____
- [ ] _____
- [ ] _____
- [ ] _____
- [ ] _____
- [ ] _____
- [ ] _____

Important	Positive Thoughts

JAMES 5:14-15

Is anyone among you sick? Let them call the elders of the church to pray over them and anoint them with oil in the name of the Lord.

And the prayer offered in faith will make the sick person well; the Lord will raise them up. If they have sinned, they will be forgiven.

7 Monday

8 Tuesday

9 Wednesday

10 Thursday

11 Friday

12 Saturday

13 Sunday

Weekly Priorities

Top 3 goals for the week

1. _____
2. _____
3. _____

To do list

- ☐ _____
- ☐ _____
- ☐ _____
- ☐ _____
- ☐ _____
- ☐ _____
- ☐ _____
- ☐ _____
- ☐ _____
- ☐ _____
- ☐ _____
- ☐ _____
- ☐ _____
- ☐ _____
- ☐ _____
- ☐ _____
- ☐ _____

Important	Positive Thoughts

MATTHEW 6:31-33

So do not worry, saying, 'What shall we eat?' or 'What shall we drink?' or 'What shall we wear?' For the pagans run after all these things, and your heavenly Father knows that you need them. But seek first his kingdom and his righteousness, and all these things will be given to you as well.

14 Monday

15 Tuesday

16 Wednesday

17 Thursday

18 Friday

19 Saturday

20 Sunday

Weekly Priorities

Top 3 goals for the week

1. _____
2. _____
3. _____

To do list

- [ ] _____
- [ ] _____
- [ ] _____
- [ ] _____
- [ ] _____
- [ ] _____
- [ ] _____
- [ ] _____
- [ ] _____
- [ ] _____
- [ ] _____
- [ ] _____
- [ ] _____
- [ ] _____
- [ ] _____
- [ ] _____
- [ ] _____

Important	Positive Thoughts

MATTHEW 7:9-11

Which of you, if your son asks for bread, will give him a stone? Or if he asks for a fish, will give him a snake? If you, then, though you are evil, know how to give good gifts to your children, how much more will your Father in heaven give good gifts to those who ask him!

21 Monday

22 Tuesday

23 Wednesday

24 Thursday

25 Friday

26 Saturday

27 Sunday

DECEMBER 2022

Sunday	Monday	Tuesday	Wednesday
27	28	29	30
4	5	6	7
11	12	13	14
18	19	20	21
25 Christmas Day	26	27	28

DECEMBER 2022

Thursday	Friday	Saturday	Notes
1	2	3	
8	9	10	
15	16	17	
22	23	24 Christmas Eve	
29	30	31 New Year's Eve	

DECEMBER 2022

S	M	T	W	T	F	S
27	28	29	30	1	2	3
4	5	6	7	8	9	10
11	12	13	14	15	16	17
18	19	20	21	22	23	24
25	26	27	28	29	30	31

Notes

Goals & Priorities

Top 3

- ○ _____
- ○ _____
- ○ _____

Important Dates

Reminder

Health

- ○ _____
- ○ _____
- ○ _____
- ○ _____
- ○ _____

Finance

- ○ _____
- ○ _____
- ○ _____
- ○ _____
- ○ _____

Personal

- ○ _____
- ○ _____
- ○ _____
- ○ _____
- ○ _____

Career

- ○ _____
- ○ _____
- ○ _____
- ○ _____
- ○ _____

Habit Tracker

	1	2	3	4	5	6	7	8	9	10	11	12	13	14	15	16	17	18	19	20	21	22	23	24	25	26	27	28	29	30	31
____	○	○	○	○	○	○	○	○	○	○	○	○	○	○	○	○	○	○	○	○	○	○	○	○	○	○	○	○	○	○	○
____	○	○	○	○	○	○	○	○	○	○	○	○	○	○	○	○	○	○	○	○	○	○	○	○	○	○	○	○	○	○	○
____	○	○	○	○	○	○	○	○	○	○	○	○	○	○	○	○	○	○	○	○	○	○	○	○	○	○	○	○	○	○	○
____	○	○	○	○	○	○	○	○	○	○	○	○	○	○	○	○	○	○	○	○	○	○	○	○	○	○	○	○	○	○	○
____	○	○	○	○	○	○	○	○	○	○	○	○	○	○	○	○	○	○	○	○	○	○	○	○	○	○	○	○	○	○	○

Weekly Priorities

Top 3 goals for the week

1. _____

2. _____

3. _____

To do list

- ☐ _____
- ☐ _____
- ☐ _____
- ☐ _____
- ☐ _____
- ☐ _____
- ☐ _____
- ☐ _____
- ☐ _____
- ☐ _____
- ☐ _____
- ☐ _____
- ☐ _____
- ☐ _____
- ☐ _____
- ☐ _____
- ☐ _____
- ☐ _____

Important	Positive Thoughts

PSALM 103:2-5

Praise the LORD, my soul, and forget not all his benefits who forgives all your sins and heals all your diseases, who redeems your life from the pit and crowns you with love and compassion, who satisfies your desires with good things so that your youth is renewed like the eagle's.

December 2022

28 Monday

29 Tuesday

30 Wednesday

1 Thursday

2 Friday

3 Saturday

4 Sunday

Weekly Priorities

Top 3 goals for the week

1. _____

2. _____

3. _____

To do list

- [ ] _____
- [ ] _____
- [ ] _____
- [ ] _____
- [ ] _____
- [ ] _____
- [ ] _____
- [ ] _____
- [ ] _____
- [ ] _____
- [ ] _____
- [ ] _____
- [ ] _____
- [ ] _____
- [ ] _____
- [ ] _____

Important	Positive Thoughts

PSALM 107:13-16

Then they cried to the LORD in their trouble, and he saved them from their distress. He brought them out of darkness, the utter darkness, and broke away their chains. Let them give thanks to the LORD for his unfailing love and his wonderful deeds for mankind, for he breaks down gates of bronze and cuts through bars of iron.

5 Monday

6 Tuesday

7 Wednesday

8 Thursday

9 Friday

10 Saturday

11 Sunday

Weekly Priorities

Top 3 goals for the week

1. _____
2. _____
3. _____

To do list

- ☐
- ☐
- ☐
- ☐
- ☐
- ☐
- ☐
- ☐
- ☐
- ☐
- ☐
- ☐
- ☐
- ☐
- ☐
- ☐
- ☐

Important	Positive Thoughts

JOHN 14:13-16

And I will do whatever you ask in my name, so that the Father may be glorified in the Son. You may ask me for anything in my name, and I will do it. If you love me, keep my commands. And I will ask the Father, and he will give you another advocate to help you and be with you forever—

December 2022

12 Monday

13 Tuesday

14 Wednesday

15 Thursday

16 Friday

17 Saturday

18 Sunday

Weekly Priorities

Top 3 goals for the week

1. _____
2. _____
3. _____

To do list

- [ ] _____
- [ ] _____
- [ ] _____
- [ ] _____
- [ ] _____
- [ ] _____
- [ ] _____
- [ ] _____
- [ ] _____
- [ ] _____
- [ ] _____
- [ ] _____
- [ ] _____
- [ ] _____
- [ ] _____
- [ ] _____
- [ ] _____

Important	Positive Thoughts

ROMANS 15:13

May the God of hope fill you with all joy and peace as you trust in him, so that you may overflow with hope by the power of the Holy Spirit.

19 Monday

20 Tuesday

21 Wednesday

22 Thursday

23 Friday

24 Saturday

25 Sunday

Weekly Priorities

Top 3 goals for the week

1. _____
2. _____
3. _____

To do list

- [ ] _____
- [ ] _____
- [ ] _____
- [ ] _____
- [ ] _____
- [ ] _____
- [ ] _____
- [ ] _____
- [ ] _____
- [ ] _____
- [ ] _____
- [ ] _____
- [ ] _____
- [ ] _____
- [ ] _____
- [ ] _____
- [ ] _____

Important	Positive Thoughts

PROVERBS 17:17

A friend loves at all times, and a brother is born for a time of adversity.

December 2022

26 Monday

27 Tuesday

28 Wednesday

29 Thursday

30 Friday

31 Saturday

1 Sunday

NOTES

NOTES

Made in the USA
Coppell, TX
10 May 2024

32256262R00090